soups

Written by Oakley Graham

Published by Top That! Publishing plc
Tide Mill Way, Woodbridge, Suffolk, IP12 1AP, UK
www.topthatpublishing.com

Contents

Contents

Super Soups

The English word "soup" originates from the Teutonic word "suppa", which refers to a medieval dish consisting of a thick stew poured onto slices of stale bread, called "sop". From its humble origins, both in the UK and across the world, soup has metamorphosed into a staple restaurant and household cuisine.

The first soup dates back to 6000 B.C., with the main ingredient being hippopotamus!

From the comfort food simplicity of tomato and chicken soup, to the more complex bouillabaisse and seafood chowder varieties, the soup recipes in this book are ideal as a nutritious starter or a main course meal. Above all, the recipes in this book have been selected to offer a diverse range of superior soup flavors, from around the world, and are made with readily available ingredients.

"Of soup and love, the first is the best." An old Spanish proverb.

Super Soups

"Troubles are easier to take with soup than without." An old Jewish saying.

Most of the recipes described in the book require a large saucepan with a covering lid and a food processor or blender. It cannot be overstressed that a good quality saucepan will not only help to prevent burning the ingredients, but it will also make the process of preparing the soups that much easier. A good quality blender is also less likely to burn out when preparing large batches of soup. Finally, some of the recipes require that you use a slow cooker. These can be bought inexpensively from all good cook shops or online.

Classic Tomato Soup

Classic Tomato Soup

You will need:

- 1 tbsp olive oil
- 1 onion, chopped
- 2 cloves garlic, peeled and chopped
- 1½ lb (750 g) quartered ripe tomatoes
- 14 oz (400 g) canned chopped tomatoes
- 1 carrot, chopped
- 34 fl.oz (1 litre) chicken stock
- salt and pepper

Serves 4

1. Sauté the onion, garlic and tomatoes in the olive oil for 5–6 minutes.

2. Add the chopped tomatoes, carrot and chicken stock and simmer for 30 minutes.

3. Purée the mixture, in batches, in a blender.

4. Season with salt and pepper.

5. Serve with crunchy garlic bread and some extra black pepper.

Top Tip!

For a vegetarian option, substitute the chicken stock with vegetable stock.

Slow-cooked Minestrone Soup

Slow-cooked Minestrone Soup

You will need:

- 25 fl.oz (750 ml) vegetable stock
- 14 oz (400 g) canned chopped tomatoes
- 14 oz (400 g) canned white (cannellini or navy) beans, drained
- 2 carrots, peeled and chopped
- 1 celery stalk, chopped
- 1 onion, chopped
- 1 oz (25 g) peas
- 1 tsp dried thyme
- ½ tsp dried sage
- 2 bay leaves
- salt and pepper to season
- 8 oz (225 g) cooked pasta (ditalini pasta is perfect, but other types can be used)
- 1 medium zucchini, chopped

Extra equipment:

- slow cooker

Serves 4–6

1. Simply add all of the ingredients to the slow cooker. Cover and cook on low for 6–8 hours or on high for 3–4 hours.

2. Serve with crusty white bread—the perfect comfort food accompaniment!

Top Tip!

Part of the beauty of this dish is that you can add any spare ingredients that you have lying around that need to be used up.

Chicken Noodle Soup

Chicken Noodle Soup

You will need:

- 35 fl.oz (1 litre) chicken stock
- 6 oz (175 g) boneless chicken breast (remove any skin)
- 1 tsp fresh root ginger, chopped
- 1 garlic clove, finely chopped
- 2 oz (50 g) noodles
- 2 tbsp frozen or canned sweet corn
- 3 large mushrooms, thinly sliced
- 3 carrots, thinly sliced
- 2 tsp soy sauce
- sprig of parsley to garnish
- small finely sliced chili to garnish (optional)

Serves 4

1. Pour the chicken stock, chicken breast, ginger and garlic into a pan and bring to the boil.

2. Cover the pan and reduce the heat. Simmer for 20 minutes, until the chicken is tender.

3. Remove the chicken and shred into small pieces.

4. Return the chicken to the pan and add the noodles, sweet corn, mushrooms, carrots and the soy sauce.

5. Simmer for a further 4 minutes, or until the noodles are cooked.

6. Serve sprinkled with parsley and a garnish of finely sliced chili (optional).

Leek and Potato Soup

Leek and Potato Soup

You will need:

- 1 tbsp oil
- 12 oz (350 g) potatoes, peeled and sliced
- 3 large leeks, washed and finely sliced
- 1¼ pt (700 ml) vegetable stock
- 10 fl.oz (300 ml) milk
- freshly ground black pepper
- light cream (optional)

Serves 6

1. First, heat the oil in a saucepan and fry the potato and leeks, until soft but not colored.

2. Next, add the stock and cook until the potatoes are tender.

3. Add the mixture to a blender and process until smooth. Then, return to the saucepan and add the milk.

4. Garnish with sprigs of parsley.

Top Tip!
Serve with a swirl of light cream for an additional decorative flourish.

Pumpkin Soup

Pumpkin Soup

You will need:

- 1 oz (25 g) butter
- 2 lb (900 g) pumpkin (peeled, seeds removed and chopped)
- 1 large onion (roughly chopped)
- 1 large potato (peeled and chopped)
- 1 large carrot (peeled and chopped)
- 1 stick celery (chopped and thick strings discarded)
- 1¼ pt (700 ml) vegetable stock
- salt and pepper to taste
- 10 fl.oz (300 ml) light cream
- sour cream (optional)
- 2 tbsp of chopped chives to garnish

Serves 6

1. Melt the butter in a saucepan and add the vegetables.

2. Cook gently for 5 minutes, stirring occasionally. Don't allow the vegetables to brown.

3. Pour in the vegetable stock and stir.

4. Simmer gently until the vegetables are just cooked (approx 20 minutes) and then purée with an electric blender.

5. Return the puréed vegetables to the saucepan and season to taste.

6. Add the light cream and heat the soup to serving temperature.

7. Add a swirl of sour cream and sprinkle with the chopped chives to garnish.

8. Serve with fresh, crusty rolls.

Rustic Vegetable Soup

Rustic Vegetable Soup

You will need:

- 2 lb, 2 oz (1 kg) mixed root vegetables, such as carrots, celery, leeks, parsnips, turnips (or rutabaga), potatoes, onions, swedes
- 3 oz (75 g) butter
- 2 garlic cloves, peeled and thinly sliced
- 1 bay leaf
- salt and black pepper to taste
- 10 fl.oz (300 ml) vegetable stock
- small celery stick or scallions to garnish

Serves 6

1. Wash and prepare the vegetables and slice them into bite-sized pieces.

2. Heat the butter in a large pan and add the vegetables, garlic, bay leaf, and a little salt and black pepper.

3. Stir well, then cover and simmer for 15 minutes, stirring occasionally.

4. Add the vegetable stock, bring to the boil, then cover and simmer gently for another 30 minutes or until the vegetables are tender.

5. Remove the bay leaf. Strain the soup, keeping the liquid.

6. Coarsely mash half of the vegetables and reintroduce to the liquid.

7. Return the remaining unmashed vegetables to the liquid.

8. Reheat the soup and add salt and pepper, according to taste.

9. Serve the rustic vegetable soup with a small celery stick or scallion garnish.

Mushroom Soup

Mushroom Soup

You will need:

- 1 oz (25 g) butter
- 1 small onion, finely chopped
- 1 small garlic clove, peeled and chopped
- 1 lb (450 g) mushrooms, (your favorite variety), chopped, reserving a few for the garnish
- 1 slice of bread, crusts removed
- 1¾ pt (1 litre) chicken or vegetable stock
- salt and freshly ground black pepper
- a pinch of nutmeg
- parsley stalks, bashed with a rolling pin and tied with kitchen string
- 2 tbsp fresh chopped parsley (to garnish)

Serves 4

1. Melt the butter in a large heavy-based saucepan. Add the onion, sweat (cook gently without coloring the onions) for 10 minutes.

2. Add the garlic and the mushrooms and cook slowly for 10 minutes, stirring while they soften. Crumble in the bread and stir again to combine.

3. Add the stock, seasoning, nutmeg and tied parsley stalks (this way you get the flavor without the annoying bits of stalk) and bring to the boil. Simmer for 10 minutes.

4. Remove the parsley stalks and string, liquidize and sieve the soup if you want. This is not necessary if you want a rustic finish.

5. When you are ready to serve, re-heat the soup. Garnish with parsley and a few extra mushrooms to finish.

French Onion Soup

French Onion Soup

You will need:

- 3 tbsp olive oil
- 4 large white onions, thinly-sliced
- 3 garlic cloves, peeled and chopped
- 1 tsp salt
- 1 tsp mustard powder
- pinch of dried thyme
- 1 pt (600 ml) vegetable stock
- 2 tsp soy sauce
- 1 glass of red wine (optional)
- ½ tsp white pepper
- 6 slices of thick white bread (cut into squares)
- 10 oz (280 g) grated Gruyère cheese

Serves 6

1. Heat the olive oil on a medium heat. Then, add the onions, garlic and salt and cook for 10 minutes, stirring occasionally.

2. Add the mustard and thyme, stir well and simmer over a very low heat for 35 minutes.

3. Add the vegetable stock, soy sauce, red wine and white pepper. Simmer for another 10 minutes.

4. Ladle the soup into stoveproof bowls and top with bread squares followed by the grated Gruyère cheese.

5. Place the bowls under the grill in order to melt and brown the cheese and bread squares.

Zucchini Soup

Zucchini Soup

You will need:

- 1 tbsp butter
- 1 medium onion, chopped
- 1 clove garlic, peeled and crushed
- 1 medium carrot, shredded
- 2 medium zucchini, sliced or chopped
- 2 apples, peeled and diced
- 1 pt (600 ml) chicken stock
- 2 tsp curry powder
- salt and pepper, to taste
- 6 tbsp light cream

Serves 6

1. Melt the butter over low heat in a large saucepan. Then, sauté the onion, garlic and carrot until the ingredients begin to yellow.

2. Add the zucchini, diced apple, chicken stock, and curry powder. Boil for 2 minutes. Then, reduce the heat to low, cover, and simmer for a further 20 minutes.

3. Allow the soup to cool and then purée in a blender in small batches.

4. Return the soup to the saucepan and reheat. Add salt and pepper to taste.

5. Serve with a decorative twirl of light cream.

Carrot Soup

Carrot Soup

You will need:

- 2 tbsp butter
- 8 medium carrots, peeled and sliced
- 1 onion, finely chopped
- 1 pt (600 ml) vegetable stock
- 3 tbsp white rice, washed
- salt and freshly ground pepper
- parsley to garnish

Serves 6

1. Melt the butter in a large saucepan. Then, add the carrots and onions and stir until they are coated with butter.

2. Cover the pan and cook on a low heat for 10 minutes, adding a little water after 5 minutes in order to prevent the vegetables from burning.

3. Next, add the vegetable stock and white rice. Cover and cook for a further 20 minutes.

4. Purée the soup in a food processor. Then, return the soup to the pan and reheat.

5. Season with salt and pepper and serve with a garnish of parsley.

Broccoli Cheese Soup

Broccoli Cheese Soup

You will need:

- 1 lb (450 g) fresh broccoli
- 6 oz (175 g) mature cheddar cheese, grated
- 6 oz (175 g) potatoes
- 1 medium onion, peeled
- 1¼ pt (700 ml) chicken stock
- 1 tbsp sunflower oil
- pinch of salt and pepper
- ½ tsp white sugar

Serves 4

1. Chop the onion, potatoes and broccoli (put half of the broccoli florets to one side).

2. Pour the chicken stock into a large saucepan and bring it to the boil.

3. Heat the oil into a second large saucepan. Then, fry the onion until soft and add the potatoes.

4. Next, add the boiling chicken stock and sugar, and cook the potatoes and onions for about 10 minutes.

5. Add half of the broccoli, and cook until tender. Add salt and pepper to taste.

6. Pour the soup into a blender, with the majority of the uncooked broccoli florets and process until smooth.

7. Return the soup back into the saucepan, and stir in the grated cheddar cheese.

8. Serve with a garnish of uncooked broccoli florets (optional).

Homemade Chicken Soup

Homemade Chicken Soup

You will need:

- I tbsp olive oil
- I large onion, chopped
- I large carrot, chopped
- I stalk of celery, chopped
- 2 cloves of garlic, peeled and finely chopped
- salt and pepper to taste
- chopped fresh parsley, sage, rosemary and thyme
- 6 oz (175 g) boneless chicken breast (remove any skin), cut into thin strips
- 27 fl.oz (750 ml) chicken stock
- sprig of parsley to garnish

Serves 4

1. Heat up the olive oil in a large saucepan on a medium heat.

2. Add the chopped vegetables and a pinch of salt and pepper. After a couple of minutes, add the garlic. Cook the vegetables for 10 minutes, or until they are soft.

3. Next, add the sage, rosemary and thyme and cook for a further two minutes.

4. Then, add the chicken pieces and cook for another two minutes.

5. Add the chicken stock.

6. Bring the soup to a boil, then reduce heat to low. Simmer for 8–10 minutes.

7. Pour the soup into a blender and process until smooth.

8. Garnish with a sprig of parsley and serve with fresh, crusty bread.

Seafood Chowder

Seafood Chowder

You will need:

- 1 lb (450 g) haddock fillets, or other firm fresh fish, free from bones and skin
- 9 oz (250 g) potatoes, peeled and diced
- 1 stick of celery, chopped finely
- 1 onion, chopped
- 1 tbsp dried parsley
- 1 tbsp dried rosemary, crushed
- salt and pepper to season
- Tabasco or other hot sauce to taste
- 17 fl.oz (500 ml) white wine
- 8 fl.oz (250 ml) fish stock
- 12 oz (375 g) mixed shellfish—mussels, clams, shrimps
- 3 fl.oz (100 ml) heavy cream
- 3 tbsp melted butter
- 3 tbsp plain flour

Extra equipment:

- slow cooker

Serves 6

Note: *You can add just about any type of seafood to this recipe to suit your tastes; clams, shrimp, scallops, etc. Additionally, you can add some sweet corn if you like. If you like a little extra spice, try a dash or two of chili powder.*

1. Cut the fish fillets into pieces, then place them into the slow cooker, along with the potatoes, celery and onion.
2. Add the parsley, rosemary and salt and pepper to season. Gently mix them in with the fish.
3. Add the hot sauce to taste, along with the white wine and fish stock.
4. Stir gently again, then cover and cook on high for 4 hours or on low for 8 hours.
5. About an hour before your seafood chowder is finished cooking add the mixed shellfish. Next, blend together the heavy cream, melted butter and the flour, making sure it is mixed well. Gently stir it into the chowder and continue to cook.
6. Serve with fresh bread.

Rustic Chickpea and Pasta Soup

Rustic Chickpea and Pasta Soup

You will need:

- 1 tbsp olive oil
- 1 onion, finely chopped
- 2 cloves garlic, peeled and crushed
- 4 oz (100 g) pancetta or thin streaky bacon, cut into small strips
- 1 lb, 12 oz (800 g) canned chickpeas
- 4–5 large, juicy tomatoes, skinned and chopped
- 1 tsp dried mixed herbs
- 20 fl.oz (600 ml) vegetable or chicken stock
- 3 oz (75 g) small conchiglie pasta
- 2 bay leaves
- salt and ground black pepper
- 2–3 tbsp fresh parsley, chopped

Serves 4

1. Heat the oil in a large pan over a medium heat. Add the onion and garlic and cook for 5 minutes until soft. Add the pancetta or bacon and cook for a further 5 minutes.

2. Drain the chickpeas and reserve 5 fl.oz (150 ml) of the liquid. Put half of the chickpeas in a bowl and mash with a fork. Add to the pan with the rest of the chickpeas, together with the tomatoes, mixed herbs, stock and reserved chickpea liquid. Add the conchiglie pasta and bay leaves, stirring to separate the pasta. Bring to the boil, lower the heat and cook for a further 10–15 minutes until the pasta is cooked.

3. Remove the bay leaves, season with salt and pepper and serve sprinkled with parsley and drizzled with a little extra olive oil.

Spicy Sausage and Chickpea Soup

Spicy Sausage and Chickpea Soup

You will need:

- 1 large pinch saffron strands (optional)
- 2 tbsp olive oil
- 8 oz (225 g) mini chorizo sausage or similar, cut into small cubes
- ½ tsp dried chili flakes
- 2 garlic cloves, peeled and finely chopped
- 14 oz (400 g) canned chopped tomatoes
- a pinch of sugar
- 14 oz (400 g) canned chickpeas, drained
- 10 oz (280 g) new potatoes, quartered lengthways
- 1 bay leaf
- 1¾ pt (1 litre) vegetable stock
- salt and pepper
- 4 tbsp flat-leaf parsley, freshly chopped (save a few leaves to garnish)
- chili oil (to serve)

Serves 4

1. Soak the saffron (if using) in a little warm water and set aside for 10 minutes. Meanwhile, heat the oil in a large pan, add the sausage and cook for 2–3 minutes until golden brown. Drain and set aside.

2. Add the chili flakes and garlic to the pan. Cook for 1–2 minutes. Stir in the tomatoes, sugar, chickpeas, potatoes, bay leaf, stock, saffron with its liquid and the sausage.

3. Bring to the boil, reduce the heat and simmer for 30 minutes with a lid on, stirring occasionally until the potatoes are cooked through and the mixture thickens slightly. Season with salt and pepper.

4. Stir in most of the fresh parsley and spoon into individual soup bowls. Drizzle with a little chili oil, sprinkle with the remaining parsley and serve with plenty of crusty bread.

Beef Consommé with Peas

Beef Consommé with Peas

You will need:

- 2 pt (1.2 litres) clear beef stock or use a stock cube
- 3 oz (75 g) anellini pasta
- 4 oz (100 g) frozen peas
- salt and freshly ground black pepper

Serves 4

1. Bring the stock to a gentle boil in a large saucepan.

2. Add the pasta, stir once, bring back to the boil and simmer gently until the pasta is al dente (cooked, but still firm).

3. Add the peas in the last minute or two. Stir again to prevent the pasta sticking. Season with salt and pepper to finish, then serve.

Chicken and Asparagus Soup

Chicken and Asparagus Soup

You will need:

- 2 skinless chicken breasts
- 5 fl.oz (150 ml) dry white wine
- 5 fl.oz (150 ml) chicken stock
- 5 fl.oz (150 ml) water
- 2 bay leaves
- sprig fresh rosemary
- a few black peppercorns
- 2 tbsp olive oil
- 1 large onion, finely chopped
- 1 clove garlic, peeled and crushed
- 2 carrots, cut into thin strips
- 6 oz (150 g) fine asparagus, cut into pieces 1 in. (2.5 cm) long
- 3 oz (75 g) capellini pasta
- ½ tsp dried oregano
- 2 tbsp chopped fresh parsley
- salt and pepper

Serves 4–6

1. Put the chicken breasts, wine, chicken stock, water, bay leaves, rosemary and peppercorns into a large saucepan. Bring to the boil, lower the heat and cover the pan. Cook for about 20–25 minutes until the chicken breasts are cooked through. Drain through a sieve, reserving the liquid. When cool enough to handle, cut the chicken into small pieces, discarding the rest of the contents of the sieve.

2. Heat the oil in a large pan over a medium heat. Add the onion, garlic and carrot and cook for 5–8 minutes until golden brown. Add the asparagus, capellini pasta, oregano and cooked chicken. Add enough water to the reserved liquid to make 1 pt (600 ml), then pour it over the contents of the pan. Bring to the boil, lower the heat and simmer gently until the asparagus and pasta are cooked. Sprinkle with parsley and season with salt and pepper before serving.

Florentine Pea and Spinach Soup

Florentine Pea and Spinach Soup

You will need:

- 2 oz (50 g) butter
- 1 onion, finely chopped
- 2 cloves garlic, peeled and crushed
- 1 carrot, finely chopped
- 1½ pt (900 ml) vegetable stock
- ½ tsp dried mint
- 8 oz (225 g) baby spinach leaves
- 2 oz (50 g) pecorino cheese, grated
- 8 oz (225 g) frozen peas
- 2 oz (50 g) malloreddus pasta
- 4 tbsp heavy cream
- 3–4 large basil leaves torn in shreds
- salt and black pepper
- fresh rosemary sprigs to garnish

Serves 4–6

1. Melt the butter in a large pan over a medium heat. Add the onion, garlic and carrot and cook gently for 4–5 minutes until golden. Add the stock and the mint, bring to the boil and simmer for 5–6 minutes.

2. Add the spinach leaves, cheese and three-quarters of the peas. Cook for a further 2–3 minutes until the peas are cooked. Remove from the heat and allow the soup to cool a little. Put the soup into a blender or food processor and whizz until very smooth. Return to the pan.

3. Put the pan back over a low heat, and add the malloreddus pasta. Cook for 4–5 minutes before adding the rest of the peas. Simmer gently for a minute or two, then stir in the cream and basil and season with salt and black pepper. Garnish with fresh sprigs of rosemary.

Italian Meatball Soup

Italian Meatball Soup

You will need:

- 12 oz (340 g) extra lean beef mince
- 2 eggs, beaten
- 2 oz (50 g) fine dry breadcrumbs
- 2 fl. oz (60 ml) milk
- 2 tbsp grated Parmesan cheese
- salt and pepper to season
- 1 tsp garlic powder
- 4 carrots, peeled and sliced
- 1 lb (450 g) potatoes, chopped
- 10 fl.oz (300 ml) water
- ¼ tsp oregano
- ¼ tsp basil
- 10 fl.oz (300 ml) beef stock
- 1 lb (450 g) vegetables, including zucchini and red and yellow peppers, sliced

Extra equipment:

- slow cooker

Serves 4

1. Mix the first seven ingredients together in a large bowl. Scoop the mixture together to form firm meatballs and set aside on a plate, in the refrigerator.

2. Next, brown the meatballs in a shallow pan, then place the carrots and potatoes in the slow cooker and place the meatballs on top.

3. Combine the water, oregano, basil, beef stock, and pour over the meatballs.

4. Cover and cook on low for 4–6 hours. Add the vegetables and turn the slow cooker to high. Cover and continue to cook for another hour, or until the vegetables are tender.

Asparagus Soup

Asparagus Soup

You will need:

- 25 asparagus heads
- 1 oz (25 g) butter
- 1 small onion, finely chopped
- 2 tsp plain flour
- 1¾ pt (1 litre) vegetable stock
- 8 fl.oz (240 ml) light cream

Serves 4

1. Clean and chop the asparagus.

2. Heat the butter in a large saucepan and gently fry the onion.

3. Sprinkle the flour onto the asparagus and place them into the saucepan.

4. Add a small amount of the vegetable stock and stir continuously for 2–3 minutes.

5. Then, add the rest of the stock and bring the soup to the boil.

6. Simmer the soup for 45 minutes and remove from the heat.

7. Allow the soup to cool, then transfer it to a blender. Blend the soup until is smooth.

8. Season with salt and pepper and add the cream.

9. Re-heat the soup, without boiling, and serve.

Spinach Soup

Spinach Soup

You will need:

- 2 tbsp olive oil
- 2 large onions, peeled and chopped
- 3 cloves of garlic, peeled and chopped
- 2 large potatoes, peeled and diced
- 1¾ pt (1 litre) chicken stock
- 9 oz (250 g) baby spinach
- salt and freshly ground black pepper
- 4 tbsp heavy cream
- fresh parsley to garnish

Serves 4

1. Heat the oil in a large saucepan and gently cook the onions, with 1 tsp of salt, until soft.

2. Next, add the garlic and diced potatoes and stir continuously for 2 minutes.

3. Then, add the chicken stock and bring to the boil. Next, reduce the heat and simmer for 15 minutes.

4. Add the baby spinach and simmer for a further 5 minutes.

5. Season with salt and freshly ground black pepper, then remove from the heat.

6. When cool, transfer the soup to a blender and process.

7. Reheat the soup and add the heavy cream just prior to serving.

8. Garnish with fresh parsley.

Cauliflower Soup

Cauliflower Soup

You will need:

- 1 tbsp olive oil
- 2½ pt (1½ litres) vegetable stock
- 1 medium onion, chopped
- 2 cloves garlic, peeled and chopped
- 1 large cauliflower, cut into florets
- 1 large potato, peeled and diced
- 4 tbsp crème fraîche
- 9 oz (250 g) Stilton cheese (or your favorite strong, crumbly cheese)
- salt and black pepper
- fresh basil

Serves 4–6

1. Heat the olive oil in a large saucepan, then gently cook the onion and garlic until softened.

2. Add the bay leaf and 2½ pt (1½ litres) of cold vegetable stock, followed by the potato and cauliflower.

3. Bring to the boil, then reduce the heat and simmer for 20 minutes until the vegetables are tender.

4. Remove the soup from the heat and allow to cool. Then, transfer to a blender and purée the soup.

5. Return the soup to the pan and add the crème fraîche and the Stilton (crumble the cheese into the soup).

6. Reheat the soup, without boiling, so the cheese melts and season with salt and black pepper.

7. Serve with a fresh basil garnish.

Classic Watercress Soup

Classic Watercress Soup

You will need:

- 3 tbsp olive oil
- 1 large onion, finely chopped
- 9 oz (250 g) celeriac (celery root), peeled and cut into chunks
- 1¾ pt (1 litre) vegetable stock
- 7 oz (200 g) fresh watercress, hard stems removed
- salt and black pepper
- fresh herb garnish (optional)
- sour cream (optional)

Serves 4

1. Heat the olive oil in a large saucepan and fry the onion until softened.

2. Add the celeriac and fry for 4 minutes.

3. Now add the vegetable stock and bring the soup to the boil. Then, reduce the heat and simmer for 20 minutes, or until the celeriac is soft.

4. Next, add the watercress and immediately remove from the heat.

5. When the soup has cooled, transfer it to a blender and process it into a purée.

6. Return the soup to the pan and heat to serving temperature.

7. Season with salt and peper and serve with sour cream and a fresh herb garnish of your choice.

Tomato Curry Soup

Tomato Curry Soup

You will need:

- 14 oz (400 g) canned chopped tomatoes
- 1 tsp salt
- 2 tsp chili powder
- 1 tsp ground coriander
- 3 tbsp oil
- 1 tsp white cumin seeds
- ½ tsp black mustard seeds
- 1 tsp ground fenugreek
- 1 tsp garlic, finely grated
- 1 tsp ginger, finely grated
- 7 fl.oz (200 ml) coconut milk
- 2 tbsp lemon juice
- paneer or 1 tbsp heavy cream, to garnish

Extra equipment:

- pestle and mortar

Serves 3–4

1. Place the canned tomatoes in a large mixing bowl. Add the salt, one teaspoon of the chili powder and the ground coriander and mix together.

2. Heat the oil in a saucepan. Grind the cumin and mustard seeds in a pestle and mortar. Add these, the fenugreek and the remaining chili powder and stir-fry for 30 seconds.

3. Add the garlic and ginger and cook for a minute on a moderate heat. Remove from the heat and add the tomato mixture. Return to a medium heat and cook the mixture for 3–4 minutes.

4. Add the coconut milk and reduce the heat. Simmer with the lid on for 4–5 minutes, stirring occasionally. Check and adjust the seasoning to taste.

5. Add the lemon juice to the pan and garnish with cream or paneer pieces.

Apple and Leek Soup

Apple and Leek Soup

You will need:

- ½ oz (15 g) butter
- 4 tsp curry powder (adjust according to taste)
- 3 leeks, chopped
- 1 large potato, peeled and diced
- 2 large Granny Smith apples, peeled, cored and chopped
- 1½ pt (850 ml) vegetable stock
- salt and pepper to taste
- 2 fl.oz (60 ml) plain natural yogurt
- sprig of thyme to garnish

Serves 4

1. Melt the butter in a medium-sized saucepan. Then add the curry powder, stirring continuously so it doesn't burn.

2. After one minute, add the leeks, potato, and apples and cook for 5 minutes on a medium heat.

3. Pour in vegetable stock and bring the soup to a boil. Then cover the saucepan, reduce the heat and simmer the soup for 30 minutes.

4. Remove the soup from the heat and allow to cool. Then, purée the soup in a blender to obtain a smooth consistency.

5. Return the soup to the pan and reheat. Season with salt and pepper, according to taste, and serve with a swirl of plain yogurt and a sprig of thyme.

Gazpacho Soup

Gazpacho Soup

You will need:

- 1 red pepper, hulled and de-seeded
- 1 cucumber, skinned and de-seeded
- 6 ripe tomatoes, de-seeded
- 14 oz (400 g) canned chopped tomatoes
- half an onion, peeled and diced
- 1 green pepper hulled and de-seeded
- 4 tbsp extra virgin olive oil
- 3 cloves of garlic, peeled and crushed
- 4 tbsp of red wine vinegar
- salt and pepper
- watercress (for the garnish)

For the croutons:

- 1 oz (25 g) butter
- 3 slices bread (crusts removed), cut into ½ in. cubes
- salt and pepper
- 1 tbsp olive oil

Serves 4

1. Blend half of the red pepper and half of the cucumber, along with the ripe tomatoes, canned tomatoes, onion, green pepper, olive oil, garlic and the red wine vinegar.

2. Add salt and pepper, according to taste.

3. Sieve the liquid into a large bowl and place in a refrigerator for at least one hour.

4. When the soup has cooled, ladle portions into pre-chilled bowls.

5. Add the remaining chopped red pepper and cucumber to each bowl.

6. Garnish with the watercress and croutons.

For the croutons

Heat the butter in a shallow pan and add the bread cubes, seasoning and olive oil. Fry gently until golden brown on all sides, remove from the pan and drain on kitchen towel.

Chicken Tortilla Soup

Chicken Tortilla Soup

You will need:

- 2 tbsp olive oil
- 1 lb (450 g) chicken breasts, sliced
- 1 small onion, chopped
- 2 cloves garlic, peeled and finely chopped
- 1 tbsp cumin powder
- ½ tsp chipotle powder
- 2 tsp chili powder
- 8 oz (225 g) cream cheese
- 2 x 14 oz (400 g) canned chopped tomatoes
- 1 pt (600 ml) chicken broth
- 2 tsp salt
- 1 avocado, peeled and sliced
- 1 large packet plain tortilla crisps
- 6–8 lime wedges, depending on the number of servings (optional)

Serves 6–8

1. Heat the oil in a large saucepan and then brown the chicken strips with the chopped onion and the garlic.

2. Add the cumin, chipotle and chili powder and cook for 2–3 minutes, stirring continuously.

3. Next, add the cream cheese, a spoonful at a time. Using the back of a spoon, blend the cheese into the mixture.

4. Stir in the remaining ingredients, breaking up a few of the crisps, and heat through.

5. Serve with a slice of avocado on top and a bowl of plain tortilla crisps (for dipping into the soup). A wedge of lime (to squeeze on top) and a sprinkling of parsley make perfect additions to this flavorsome soup.

Beef and Vegetable Soup

Beef and Vegetable Soup

You will need:

- 2 tbsp olive oil
- 5 oz (150 g) stewing beef, cut into rough chunks
- 1 large onion, peeled and finely chopped
- 1 tsp thyme, finely chopped
- ½ tbsp plain flour
- 2 tsp tomato purée
- 2 tbsp beef extract, dissolved in 3½ pt (2 litres) of hot water
- 2 large carrots, peeled and cut into rough chunks
- 3 sticks of celery, cut into rough chunks
- 1 large parsnip (optional), peeled and cut into chunks
- 3 leaves of red cabbage, cut into rough chunks
- salt and pepper

Serves 4–6

1. Heat the oil in a saucepan. Then, fry the stewing beef for 3–4 minutes until browned. Add salt and pepper.

2. Lower the heat before adding the onions and thyme and gently cook until soft.

3. Next, stir in the plain flour and tomato purée.

4. Gradually stir in the beef extract stock and bring to the boil.

5. Add more salt and pepper and simmer the soup for one hour.

6. Then, add the carrots, celery and parsnip and cook for a further 20 minutes.

7. When the beef is tender, add the red cabbage and simmer for another 10 minutes before serving.

Oxtail Soup

Oxtail Soup

You will need:

- 1 oxtail (from your local butcher)
- 1 tbsp seasoned flour
- 4 tbsp olive oil
- 4 pt (2¼ litres) vegetable stock
- 1 tsp salt
- 3 tbsp parsley, finely chopped
- 1 bay leaf
- 2 large carrots, diced
- 1 small turnip, diced
- 1 medium onion, diced
- light cream (optional)

Serves 6

1. Cut the oxtail into small joints and roll in the seasoned flour.

2. Heat the oil in a large saucepan and fry the joints until brown.

3. Remove any excess fat and add the vegetable stock, salt, chopped parsley and the bay leaf.

4. Cover the pan and simmer for 2 hours.

5. Remove the pan from the heat and leave to go cold. Then, remove any solidified fat.

6. Add the vegetables and bring the soup to the boil. Simmer for a further 2½ hours.

7. Remove bones and transfer the soup to a blender when cooled. Blend the soup to achieve a smooth consistency.

8. When you are ready to serve, season with salt and pepper, and garnish with parsley and light cream.

Dutch Mustard Soup

Dutch Mustard Soup

You will need:

- 5 oz (150 g) bacon
- 2 tbsp oil
- 2 tbsp wholegrain mustard
- 1 onion, finely chopped
- 1¾ pt (1 litre) chicken stock
- 4 fl.oz (125 ml) crème fraîche
- 4½ oz (125 g) smeerkase cheese (or alternative spreadable cheese)
- 4 tbsp cornstarch
- salt and pepper

Serves 4

1. Cut the bacon into small squares and fry in a shallow pan until crisp. Remove the bacon from the pan and place onto a piece of kitchen towel in order to remove excess oil.

2. Heat the oil in a different pan and then sauté the onion.

3. Add the mustard to the onion and then gradually add the chicken stock to the mixture, stirring continuously. Bring the chicken stock to the boil and then add the crème fraîche and cheese.

4. Stir until smooth and then add the cornstarch.

5. When the soup thickens, add salt and pepper to taste.

6. Garnish with green herbs of your choice and serve with the crispy diced bacon on the side.

Mulligatawny Soup

Mulligatawny Soup

You will need:

- 2 oz (50 g) butter
- 1 onion, chopped
- 2 stalks celery, chopped
- 1 carrot, diced
- 1½ tbsp plain flour
- 1½ tbsp curry powder
- ½ apple, peeled, cored and chopped
- 1¾ pt (1 litre) chicken stock
- 4 tbsp basmati rice
- salt and pepper
- 1 pinch dried thyme
- 4 fl.oz (100 ml) heavy cream
- saffron strands for garnish (optional)

Serves 6

1. Melt the butter in a large saucepan and add the chopped onions, celery and carrot. Cook the onions on a low heat, for 3–4 minutes, until they are soft.

2. Next, add the flour, thyme and curry powder and cook for a further 2–3 minutes, stirring frequently.

3. Add the grated apple and stir on a high heat for another 3–4 minutes.

4. Add the chicken stock and simmer until the soup thickens. Then, add the rice. Keep the saucepan on a high heat until the rice is cooked and then season with salt and pepper, according to taste.

5. Add the cream, blend in a food processor until smooth and garnish.

Chicken Chive Soup

Chicken Chive Soup

You will need:

- 1 tbsp unsalted butter
- 1 tbsp chopped scallions
- 1 large potato, peeled and diced
- salt and pepper
- 2 oz (60 g) chopped garlic chives (reserve 6 buds for garnish)
- 8 fl.oz (240 ml) chicken stock
- 2 cooked chicken breasts, cut into large pieces
- 1 tbsp sour cream

Serves 4

1. In a saucepan, sauté the scallions in butter over a medium heat. Add the potato and season with salt and pepper.

2. Stir in the garlic chives and add the chicken stock. Bring to a boil, then reduce the heat and gently simmer for 10 minutes or until the potato is very tender.

3. Purée in a blender until smooth, then stir in the cooked chicken and cream. Garnish with reserved chive buds.

Ramson Soup

Ramson Soup

You will need:

- 1 oz (25 g) butter
- 1 onion, finely chopped
- 1 oz (25 g) plain flour
- 25 fl.oz (750 ml) vegetable stock
- 8 fl.oz (240 ml) light cream
- 5 tbsp ramson leaves, chopped
- salt and white pepper

Serves 4

1. Melt the butter in a large saucepan. Then, sauté the onion, until it is soft, and add the flour, stirring continuously.

2. Now pour in the vegetable stock, half of the cream and the chopped ramson.

3. Bring the soup to a boil and simmer for 10–15 minutes and remove from the heat.

4. When cool, blend the soup in a food processor to achieve a smooth consistency.

5. Return the soup to the pan and season with salt and pepper. Reheat the soup to serving temperature.

6. Finally, ladle the soup into bowls and stir the remaining cream into each serving.

Boston Baked Bean Soup

Boston Baked Bean Soup

You will need:

- 1 tbsp olive oil
- 1 large onion, chopped
- 1 large carrot, peeled and chopped
- 2 celery sticks, chopped
- 3 rashers of smoked back bacon, diced
- 14 oz (400 g) canned Boston beans
- 11 fl.oz (330 ml) vegetable stock
- 11 fl.oz (330 ml) tomato juice
- 1 tbsp steak sauce
- ½ tsp paprika
- ½ tsp mixed herbs

Serves 4

1. Heat the olive oil in a large pan and gently fry the onion, carrot, celery, and bacon for 8–10 minutes.

2. Next, add the Boston beans, vegetable stock and tomato juice, stirring continuously.

3. After 2 minutes, add a splash of steak sauce and the paprika and mixed herbs.

4. Cover the pan and simmer for a further 10 minutes or until the vegetables are tender.

5. Serve hot with fresh, crusty bread.

Thanksgiving Soup

Thanksgiving Soup

You will need:

- turkey leftovers
- 7 oz (200 g) leftover stuffing
- 1 large onion, peeled and diced
- 2 celery sticks, chopped
- 2 large carrots, peeled and sliced
- 2 large potatoes, peeled and chopped
- 3 bay leaves
- 1 tsp ground sage
- 1¾ pt (1 litre) vegetable stock
- 2½ pt (1½ litres) chicken stock
- salt and black pepper

Serves 8-10

1. Place the turkey leftovers, including the bones, in a large, deep pot (you may need to cut the bones in order for it to fit).

2. Add the stuffing, onion, celery, carrots, potatoes, bay leaves, sage, and both stocks—the bones should be completely submerged.

3. Bring the pot to the boil and then reduce to a medium heat. Simmer on this setting for one hour, regularly removing any froth from the surface.

4. Remove the bones from the pot and remove any remaining meat. Return the meat to the pot and discard the bones and skin.

5. Season with salt and pepper. Bring the pot to the boil and then reduce the heat and simmer for 20 minutes, stirring occasionally.

Classic Bouillabaisse

Classic Bouillabaisse

You will need:

- 2 leeks, washed and sliced lengthways
- 8 sprigs fresh tarragon
- 8 fresh sprigs flat-leaf parsley
- ½ tsp coriander seeds
- ½ tsp fennel seeds
- ½ tsp cumin seeds
- 1 tsp tomato purée
- 14 oz (400 g) canned whole tomatoes
- 2 tbsp olive oil
- 2 small onions, peeled and diced
- 4 cloves garlic, crushed
- 1 tsp sweet paprika
- 8 sun-dried tomatoes (dry, not packed in oil)
- 1 tsp saffron strands
- ½ tsp turmeric
- 2 tsp harissa (optional)
- 3 lb (1.25 kg) fish heads and bone (use fish, such as sole, snapper, or bass), washed and prepared
- 6 dried fennel branches
- peel from 3 oranges
- salt and pepper to season
- 3 lobsters (optional)
- 3 lb (1.25 kg) mussels, scrubbed and beards trimmed
- 4 lb, 4 oz (2 kg) fish fillets, such as halibut, red snapper, and monkfish, cut into pieces.

Extra equipment:

- slow cooker

Serves 6–8

Top Tip!

You can add just about any type of seafood to this recipe to suit your tastes.

1. Begin by making a "bouquet garni". Cut dark-green leek leaves into two equal lengths. Arrange the tarragon and parsley sprigs in the center of one leaf. Place the other leaf on top to enclose the tarragon and tie with kitchen string.

2. Next, heat a shallow pan over a medium heat and add the coriander, fennel and cumin seeds. Cook for 2–3 minutes, shaking the pan or stirring frequently, until toasted and fragrant. Let the seeds cool in a bowl.

Classic Bouillabaisse

3. Strain the can of whole tomatoes over a small bowl, reserving the liquid, but discarding the seeds. Place the tomatoes in a bowl with the liquid and set aside.

4. Heat the oil in a large frying pan and add the onions, garlic, and paprika. Cook until the onions become translucent. Next, add the tomato purée, whole tomatoes and their liquid, sun-dried tomatoes, saffron, turmeric, harissa and the toasted coriander, fennel and cumin seeds. Stir to combine.

5. Transfer the mixture to the slow cooker and add the fish heads and bones. Then, add the fennel, orange peel, and bouquet garni. Add enough water to just cover the fish and season. Next, skim the foam from the surface, reduce the heat and cook on low for 3–4 hours. Then, pour the stock through a sieve into a large bowl and discard solids. Return the liquid to the slow cooker and season.

6. Meanwhile, bring a large pan of cold water to a boil. Quickly add the lobster and cook for about 12 minutes. Remove the pan from the heat, drain the lobster and submerge in cold water to stop cooking. Drain again.

7. Add 8 fl. oz (250 ml) of the fish stock from the slow cooker into a large saucepan and add the same amount of water. Bring to a boil and add the mussels. Cover the pan and cook until the mussels open. Remove from the heat and discard any mussels that do not open.

8. Meanwhile, add the fish fillets to the slow cooker and cook until they are cooked through. Remove the tails and claws from the cooked lobster and crack them open, adding the meat and the mussels to the slow cooker, just long enough to warm.

Serve with rouille and crunchy bread.

Pea and Ham Soup

Pea and Ham Soup

You will need:

- 1 tbsp extra virgin olive oil
- ½ oz (15 g) butter
- 1 large onion, peeled and chopped
- 2 medium carrots, peeled and sliced
- 2 sticks of celery, trimmed and sliced
- a leftover bone from a joint of ham, plus 1½ cups extra ham
- 8 oz (225 g) green split peas
- sprig of thyme
- 1¼ pt (750 ml) vegetable stock
- salt and pepper
- 6 oz (175 g) good quality ham, shredded into small pieces
- a handful of fresh parsley to garnish

Serves 6

1. Heat the olive oil and butter in a large saucepan.

2. When melted, add the vegetables and stir. Cover the saucepan and cook on a low heat for 10 minutes so the vegetables are soft.

3. Add the ham bone, split peas and thyme.

4. Next, add the vegetable stock and bring to the boil. Skim the frothy residue from the surface of the soup and then simmer for one hour, or until the peas are soft and mushy.

5. Remove the bone and thyme and season with salt and pepper. Pour the soup into a blender and process until smooth.

6. Add the shredded ham to the soup and reheat prior to serving. Garnish with parsley.

Bean and Pearl Barley Soup

Bean and ~~Pearl Barley~~ Rice Soup

You will need:

- 9 oz (250 g) mixed beans
- 2 tbsp oil
- 1 garlic clove, chopped
- 1 large onion, chopped
- 4 oz (100 g) celeriac or 2 sticks of celery, peeled and diced
- 1 large carrot, peeled and diced
- salt and pepper to season
- 30 fl.oz (900 ml) vegetable stock
- 5 oz (125 g) ~~pearl barley~~ rice
- 1 red pepper, sliced
- 1 medium potato, diced

Extra equipment:

- slow cooker

Serves 2–4

1. Prepare the mixed beans by soaking them in 17 fl.oz (500 ml) of water for 8–24 hours. Drain and place into the slow cooker.

2. Heat a tablespoon of oil in a large saucepan and add the garlic, onion and celeriac. Cook for a minute or two. Add the carrot and season with salt and pepper.

3. Next, transfer the mixture into the slow cooker and stir in the stock, pearl barley, pepper and potato.

4. Cover and cook on low for 5–6 hours, or until the beans are soft.

5. Remove half of the vegetables and beans to a blender or processor, purée and return to the pan. Add more water to produce a thick soup.

6. Serve piping hot with warm, crusty bread.

Red Pepper and Tomato Soup

Red Pepper and Tomato Soup

You will need:

- 2 lb (900 g) tomatoes, halved
- 2 red peppers, quartered and deseeded
- 1 medium red onion, finely sliced
- 1 garlic clove
- 2 tbsp olive oil
- 1 vegetable stock cube
- 1 tbsp steak sauce
- 4 tbsp heavy cream
- 2 tbsp chopped flat leaf parsley

Serves 4–6

1. Preheat the oven to 400°F / 200°C.

2. Place the tomatoes, peppers, onion and whole garlic clove in a roasting tin and drizzle over the olive oil. Toss the vegetables so that they are coated in oil. Cook in the oven for 50 minutes, turning the vegetables halfway through.

3. Next, dissolve the stock cube in 17 fl.oz (500 ml) of hot water. Purée the roasted vegetables with the stock in a blender, then pass it through a sieve to remove the tomato seeds.

4. Pour the soup into a saucepan, add the steak sauce and reheat gently. Serve with a swirl of heavy cream and chopped parsley.

Cabbage Soup

Cabbage Soup

You will need:

- 1 tbsp olive oil
- 1 clove garlic, peeled and finely chopped
- 2 small leeks, roughly chopped
- 4 rashers bacon (salted), roughly chopped
- 1 savoy cabbage, shredded
- 17 fl.oz (500 ml) chicken stock
- salt and ground black pepper

Serves 4

1. Heat the olive oil in a heavy-based saucepan, over a medium heat.

2. Add the garlic and leeks and fry for 2–3 minutes.

3. Next, add the bacon and fry for a further 4 minutes, or until the bacon is nicely browned.

4. Add the savoy cabbage and fry, stirring continuously, for 2–3 minutes, or until soft.

5. Add the chicken stock and bring to the boil. Then, reduce the heat and simmer for 10 minutes.

6. Season with salt and ground black pepper and serve.

Lentil and Tomato Soup

Lentil and Tomato Soup

You will need:

- 1 tbsp olive oil
- 1 large onion, finely chopped
- 14 oz (400 g) canned chopped tomatoes
- 1½ pt (900 ml) vegetable stock
- 5 oz (150 g) red lentils
- 1 carrot, peeled and chopped
- salt and pepper
- 1 scallion, chopped

Serves 4

1. Heat the oil in a shallow pan and add the onion. Fry until browned.

2. Next, add the tomatoes, vegetable stock, lentils and carrot.

3. Bring to the boil and simmer for 30 minutes.

4. Season generously with salt and ground black pepper. Then, pour into a blender and process until smooth.

5. Serve with a garnish of chopped scallions.

Your Own Recipes